MW01505738

HEROINES

OF THE

AMERICAN REVOLUTION

⊂—◦◆◦—⊃

IDELLA BODIE

*For Selera with
wishes you enjoy
these stories of
women in the Revolution
War.* — *Idella Bodie*

SANDLAPPER PUBLISHING CO., INC.
ORANGEBURG, SOUTH CAROLINA

First Edition

Published by Sandlapper Publishing Co., Inc.
        Orangeburg, South Carolina 29115

Manufactured in the United States of America

ISBN 0-87844-170-0

Library of Congress Cataloging-in-Publication Data

Acknowledgement

I wish to acknowledge Mollie Somerville,
Historical Researcher for the National Society,
Daughters of the American Revolution,
for her outstanding research in preparation for
Women and the American Revolution.

To The Young Reader

Women played important roles on the home front and the battlefield during the American Revolution. They shared many hardships and some of the dangers.

While husbands and sons were away fighting, British soldiers and Tories threatened women. The wives who chose to stay in their homes to try to keep them from being plundered suffered cruelty. They often slept in their clothes, jumping up at the least noise. They watched cattle and horses being stolen.

Many cringed in fear when Tories entered their homes with swords drawn to take personal possessions. Cursing, the looters jerked wedding rings from fingers and buckles from shoes. They dumped contents of trunks and cut mattresses, plundering for anything of value.

Others saw their homes burn as they fled to the forests with their children.

When the British took over large homes for their headquarters, the women who stayed had to prepare and serve meals for the enemy.

Many women nursed wounded soldiers, even turning their homes into hospitals. Others organized spinning and sewing sessions to clothe the army and raise money for supplies.

A large number carried messages, some as couriers and others as spies. Whenever they picked up news of enemy movement, they took long, dangerous rides to repeat what they heard to Patriot camps.

A few who felt they had no way to make a living for themselves followed the soldiers. They carried bushel baskets on their backs with all their possessions. These women became known as "camp followers."

A small number disguised themselves as men and fought in battle.

Whatever these colonial women did, they always encouraged their husbands and sons to have faith in the cause and to fight bravely.

The Revolutionary War changed the way society looked at women. Before this time, it was considered unladylike for women to do anything but take care of children and the home. It was even considered rude for a woman to voice her opinion. Now they began to speak more openly.

Unfortunately, many of these heroines of the Revolution have never been recognized for their contributions. History books, for the most part, do not include their brave deeds—in those that do, names are often omitted.

Chiefly, officers kept the records and wrote memoirs. Even if a few women were included, it was done with "Mrs." before their husbands' names. Because almost all of these brave deeds did not receive documentation when the event occurred but were handed down through their families, some historians consider them legends.

CONTENTS

HEROINES OF THE
AMERICAN REVOLUTION

Prudence Wright
Minute Woman

When the alarm sounded in Groton, Masschusetts, Prudence Wright's husband knew it meant the British were coming. He hurried to join the other minutemen in the Battle of Lexington and Concord.

Since the town of Groton was not far from Concord, Prudence worried the British would come to their town too. If the enemy did come, they would enter across Jewett's Bridge.

Prudence had an idea. She dressed in her husband's clothes and dashed from the house to tell other women to do the same. "Bring along anything you have to fight with," she told them.

When the wives and daughters met at Prudence's home, everyone was armed in some way—one with a pitchfork. "No one will cross Jewett's Bridge tonight," Prudence declared, "not with us guarding it."

With the sounds of the night about them, they tramped through the fields and woods. At the bridge, they hid in the tall slender grass. The sound of a horse's hoofs clattered on the wooden bridge.

In one big rush the women bounded from hiding and surrounded a rider they could tell was a British officer. The man was so taken by surprise, he did not try to flee but dismounted, as if to surrender.

Prudence lowered her voice to make it sound like a man's. "Don't think you can get away from us," she said.

The officer made no attempt to escape. One of the women tied his hands behind his back. Another said, "Let's see if he has any secret messages." Two others pulled off his boots. Secret messages fell onto the bridge.

The British officer had been tricked by farmers' wives!

"Let's take him to the stockade," Prudence said, "and turn over these messages."

Afterwards, as the women continued to guard the bridge, they laughed at how they had surprised the officer. "At least he knows now that liberty is just as important to women as it is to men."

Penelope Pagett Barker
Protestor

*"The pleasure of your company
is requested for a 'tea' party at
the home of Mrs. Elizabeth King
on the 24th of October, 1774.
Refreshments will be served.
Bring a friend."*

When Penelope Barker sent this invitation to fifty-one patriotic women, the Revolutionary War had not yet begun. The women gathered at the home of Penelope's dear friend Elizabeth in Edenton, North Carolina.

Women were just beginning to take on a new role: using their rights as American citzens. Penelope was a leader. The ladies gathered to protest the tax on tea in the colonies. They enjoyed their afternoon tea but felt it was unfair for the British to put a tax on it just because it came to America in British  ships. They also opposed the tax on imported cloth.

In fact, many of the colonists protested what they called "taxation without representation." Besides not being able to vote in elections, no one from America represented the colonies in the British parliament.

The women at the party listened to Penelope read her protest against the British taxes. Then all fifty-one signed the document.

Although Penelope's husband did not try to stop her protest, he warned her the British would not listen to what women thought.

"We do not care what the British think," she told him. "We are doing our duty."

Penelope's husband was right. The British made fun of the women and called their meeting the "Edenton Tea Party," after the Boston Tea Party from an earlier time. They published cartoons showing women signing the document and emptying their tea canisters.

Like it or not, the British could not ignore the results brought about by the ladies' actions. More than 300 women boycotted tea and cloth from Britain. Without firing a shot, these women led by Penelope Pagett Barker let the British Empire know the hands that rocked the cradle had power too.

Grace and Rachel Martin
Surprise Attackers

Indians killed Elizabeth Marshall Martin's husband. Eight years later in May of 1781 Elizabeth watched their eight sons join the Continental Army of the American Revolution.

In spite of her hardships, Elizabeth felt pride in seeing her sons go off to fight for their country. "If I were a man," she told them, "I would go with you."

When her youngest son gave his life in battle at Augusta, Georgia, Elizabeth said he could not have died for a nobler cause.

While her other sons fought the Redcoats.

their wives lived with their mother-in-law in the Martin home on a busy road. It was no secret, even to the British, that the Martins were Patriots. Yet British soldiers, as well as the Patriots, often stopped at the Martin home for a night's lodging.

One day two of the wives—Grace, William's widow, and Rachel, Barclay's wife—heard that a British courier guarded by two soldiers would be passing their home. The courier would be delivering a message to Colonel John Cruger at the Ninety Six fort in the South Carolina Up Country.

The young women decided they would dress in their husbands' clothes and force the enemy to hand over the information they carried. Seizing the message would no doubt keep one group of British and Tory soldiers from joining with another to fight against the Patriots.

When the sun hung low in the sky, Grace and Rachel disguised themselves in their husbands' clothing, stuffed their hair under the men's hats, and grabbed rifles. Instead of using the road, they hurried through the woods. At a familiar bend in the road, they hid  behind thick bushes and waited.

Soon the sun set. The moon cast weird shadows across the ground. Night creatures made screeching noises. Finally, the tramp of horses echoed up the dirt road.

When the riders rounded the bend, the young women leaped from hiding and pointed guns at the soldiers.

"Halt and raise your hands!" Rachel tried to make her voice sound deep like a man's. "We know you carry papers. Hand them over, and we'll let you go."

Taken by surprise, the startled men surrendered, and the courier gave up the message.

With their mission accomplished, the ladies freed their prisoners as promised.

With a sigh of relief, the sisters watched the soldiers turn back the way they came. Without their message, the men had no reason to continue the long journey.

The young women darted back home through the woods and slipped into their own clothing. Family members praised their bravery. Sally Clay

Martin, wife of the youngest son, Matthew, hurried to carry the message to General Greene, also camped near Ninety Six.

Shortly afterwards, Mrs. Martin answered a knock at their door. Seeing the courier and his two guards, she asked, "Did I not see you traveling by my home earlier?"

"Yes," the courier said. "But my guards and I were held up by two young rebel lads and, so quickly, we had no time to use our weapons."

Since the men seemed polite, Mrs. Martin agreed to give them lodging for the night.

The next morning they sat at the breakfast table with the "rebel lads," never suspecting they had been overpowered by these young women.

Because of the patriotism of this family, a main road through North Augusta, South Carolina, bears the name Martintown Road.

Nancy Hart
War Woman

1.

A Fiery Heroine

Nancy Hart was not a pretty woman. Big and muscular, she stood six feet tall. She had red hair and a fiery temper. Smallpox left scars on her face and she was cross-eyed.

This woman was not afraid of anyone, not even Tories or Indians. And she didn't hesitate to defend herself. Once, as she boiled soap, she saw an Indian peering between the cracks of their cabin. She threw a dipperful of the hot soap in his face.

When Elijah Clarke decided to move Patriot women across the Georgia border to safety, she refused to go. "I'll stay here and fight," she said.

Nancy was physically fit and strong. She liked to hunt and often brought home deer she killed. Antlers hung on the walls of the Harts' log cabin.

The Indians called Nancy "Wahatchee," the Indian word for "War Woman." They even named a nearby stream for her. They called it "War Woman Creek."

2.
A Close Call

Nancy and her husband, Benjamin, had six sons and two daughters. One day while Benjamin and some of their children worked in the field,

Nancy and thirteen-year-old Sukey did household chores. The next thing they knew, a group of Tory soldiers from a British camp in Augusta, Georgia, stopped at their home demanding food.

Nancy told the soldiers that Tories had taken all they had. She pointed to her turkey gobbler high stepping around the yard. "That's the only thing we got left."

One of the soldiers raised his gun and shot the gobbler. He picked it up by its legs and handed it to Nancy. "Now you've got something," he said.

Inside the cabin, the rowdy men stacked their rifles against the wall and plopped down at the table to enjoy the rum they brought along.

Nancy and Sukey cleaned the turkey and prepared it for cooking. The soldiers drank rum and bragged in loud voices about murdering Nancy's Patriot neighbor, Colonel Daly, on the way to her house. Nancy's temper flared, but she did not let it show.

In a voice loud enough for the soldiers to hear, she told Sukey to go to the spring for water. Then she whispered to her daughter to blow the conch shell kept at the spring to signal danger.

Sukey hurried along. Her father and others would hear the trumpet sound and know it meant trouble at the Hart cabin.

Before Sukey returned, Nancy began to serve the turkey. Each time she went to the table, she passed by the guns stacked against the wall. On one trip, she slipped a rifle into the folds of her skirt. With her back to the noisy group, she poked the rifle through a chink, a hole, in the wall. One after the other, she sneaked the rifles and poked each through the hole to the outside.

Suddenly a Tory saw what she was doing and

alarmed the others. All sprang to their feet. Nancy raised the rifle in her hand and took aim. "Make a move," she said, "and I'll kill you."

The men froze. Confused by her crossed eyes, they couldn't tell which one she had the gun on. Then one Tory lurched forward, reaching for the gun.

Nancy did as she promised. The gun fired and the Tory fell to the floor. The other men started toward her. She grabbed another gun and shot. A second Tory fell.

At that moment Benjamin Hart and his neighbors arrived at the cabin door. They were about to shoot the remaining men when Nancy stopped them. "Shooting's too good for them," she said.

The Patriot men took the Tories behind the cabin and hanged them from a tree. For many years afterward, storytellers pointed to the hanging limb and told the story of Nancy Hart's bravery.

3.
Later Years

Many other stories tell of Nancy's patriotism. She served as a spy for Georgia's Patriot forces. Once, she crossed the Savannah River on a raft of logs tied with grapevines to get information from enemy camps. She also showed great skill in healing wounded soldiers.

After the war, the Harts moved to Brunswick,

Georgia, where Benjamin died. Later, Nancy moved to Kentucky, where she died about 1830.

4.
Honors

Nancy Hart received many honors for her heroic actions. Her name is well known throughout Georgia. A school, city, county, creek, highway, railroad locomotive, and even a Civil War militia have been named for her. The Daughters of the American Revolution have a Nancy Hart Chapter. Her portrait hangs in the Georgia state capitol. A monument erected by the United States government near the city of Hartwell reads, "To commemorate the Heroism of Nancy Hart."

In 1932 the Elbert County Chapter of the Daughters of the American Revolution reconstructed the cabin where the Hart family lived. It is made of logs from the land and has wooden shutters over small windows. The chimney and fireplace are built of stones from the original Hart home. The log walls are chinked just the way they were when Nancy shot at renegade Indians and other unwelcome visitors.

The Hart cabin, now owned by Elbert County, Georgia, is located off Georgia Highway 17, south of Elberton in the fourteen-acre Nancy Hart Forest Park. In 1992 community donations and grants restored the cabin.

Wahatchee Creek, about a half mile from the cabin, runs steady and clear. Area Indians still think of it as War Woman Creek.

Mary Anna Gibbes
Brave Teen

Thirteen-year-old Mary Anna, one of eight Gibbes children, lived with her parents in a mansion on the Stono River on John's Island in South Carolina. During the Revolutionary War, relatives brought eight other children to take refuge in the three-story brick home.

In earlier times British soldiers visited the Gibbeses' home, called "Peaceful Retreat," as friends. After the war began, the home was not peaceful. British and Tory soldiers plundered the house, carrying off personal possessions and food, and treating Mrs. Gibbes with disrespect.

One day an old slave, who had been taken away by enemy soldiers, returned with news that British officers headed up the Stono River. They planned to make Peaceful Retreat their headquarters.

When Mrs. Gibbes spotted the sail of a British ship moving toward them, she hurried to gather the children. In spite of the oncoming night, cold temperature, and drizzling rain, she set out iwth them to a neighboring plantation.

Wet, chilled, and exhausted, the group stopped at a farmer's home for a brief rest. To her horror, Mrs. Gibbes realized John Fenwick was not with them. *In their hurry, she had left her little nephew behind!*

What could be done about it now? She couldn't leave the other children to return for him. And the youngest could never make the long walk back to Peaceful Retreat and then on to the neighbor's plantation. The roar of distant guns made them even more fearful.

About that time Mary Anna spoke up. "Mother," she said, "I will return for Cousin John."

Fear stabbed Sarah Gibbes's heart. How could she let her young daughter return to face the British soldiers? Yet, she saw no other choice.

With her mother's blessing, Mary Anna hurried along the dark path with all the speed and courage she could gather.

At first the British refused to let her into the home. Mary Anna tried to keep the tremble from her voice as she explained about her young cousin.

Finally, one of the guards let her in. She dashed through the house, searching and calling. On the third floor she found John huddled behind a bed. She put her arms around him and carried him from the house.

Outside, fire from distant shelling colored the sky. Mary Anna cuddled the small boy in her arms and ran in the direction of her neighbor's plantation. She faced the journey with the same devotion to duty as her mother.

Gun shots hit the ground, sending chunks of dirt flying in all directions. Mary Anna rushed on to join the others, dodging the dirt pellets as best she could.

When John Fenwick grew up, he became a general and served his country. He built a home called Fenwick Place, three miles from Peaceful Retreat.

Lydia Barrington Darragh
Spy

1.
Meeting Planned

By fall of 1777, British forces controlled Philadelphia, Pennsylvania. British general Howe forced Lydia Barrington Darragh's neighbor to move from her home so his officers could use it as headquarters.

Fearing spies might hang around to overhear their plans, General Howe told his officers they needed a place away from headquarters to discuss military strategy. Lieutenant Barrington was

Lydia's cousin. He suggested a room in her home.

General Howe agreed, as he felt Barrington's cousin could be trusted. He sent Major John Andre to advise the Darraghs a meeting would be held in their house at eight o'clock in the evening on December 2. Andre told Lydia to see that all members of her family were in bed before they arrived.

At the set time, Lydia let the British officers in and directed them to a room prepared for their use. She told them her husband and children had retired to their bedrooms and she would do the same.

2.

The Secret Room

Lydia could not sleep. She wondered why a meeting had to be so secretive. Finally, she slipped out of bed and crept to an adjoining room to hear what the officers were saying. She crouched down by the closed door and placed her ear near the floor.

What Lydia heard filled her with fear. In two days 5,000 soldiers would surprise Washington's troops at Whitemarsh.

Trembling, Lydia hurried back to her bed. The Darraghs were Quakers. Because of their faith, they did not believe in war. Lydia's husband, William, was a teacher. He had not volunteered to fight. Lydia and William did not want their son, Charles, to fight, but they let him make his own decision. He joined the Patriot militia.

What should she do? If she told no one, many young Patriots like Charles would die. She pondered the matter until daybreak. Whatever she decided, she would not tell her husband. He must not be involved.

3.
The Long Walk

A sudden knock at the bedroom door startled Lydia. She lay still. She must pretend to be asleep. The knock came again. And a third time. She grabbed her robe and eased the door open enough to see Major Andre.

"We are leaving," he said. "You can put out the fire and blow out the candles."

As the soldiers rode away, Lydia extinguished the fire and candles and went back to bed. But still she could not sleep.

After breakfast the next morning, she told William she needed to go to the mill in Frankfort for flour. She felt sure, she said, that she could get the pass required to travel there from her cousin.

Carrying her flour sack, she walked along the British line until she saw her cousin. Lieutenant Barrington remarked about how far she had to walk in such cold weather and issued her a pass. In moments Lydia set off.

The five miles to the mill proved difficult, especially after the snow began. At Pearson's Mill she left her flour sack and continued on her way toward Whitemarsh.

The area between Frankfort and Whitemarsh was rugged. Only the scouts for the two armies went there. Lydia found the walk long and lonely.

After several hours, she saw a horseman approaching. She was happy to see he was a Patriot, and one she knew—Lieutenant Colonel Thomas Craig of the light horse cavalry.

Feeling great relief, Lydia told the colonel she had news but he must first promise to never reveal that she told him.

He assured her only General Washington would hear the truth. Lydia then told him of the British plans for Whitemarsh she had overheard.

On her way home Lydia picked up her twenty-five-pound bag of flour. When she reached the house, she went straight to bed. But she could not sleep for worry.

The next morning she sat at her window and

watched the British soldiers marching on their way to Whitemarsh.

4.
The Walls with Ears

That evening the same British officer who had been in her home just two nights before appeared at the door. John Andre ordered Lydia to follow him to the room where the officers met.

He shut the door and turned to face her. "Were all members of your family in bed on the evening of December 2 as instructed?" he asked.

Weak with fright, Lydia assured him all had gone to bed as he ordered.

She found it hard to lie, so she was thankful he did not suspect her or ask if all stayed in their beds during the night. He was certain, he said, that she had been asleep. Had he not knocked three times before he woke her?

As he turned to leave, he said, "The walls must have ears. We have been betrayed. Our scout reported as he neared General Washington's camp he saw the cannon mounted and the troops under arms. We had no choice but to retreat like a bunch of fools."

5.

Lydia Remembered

After the war, Lydia's story became known through her daughter, Ann, and other women. It was also written up in a journal of Elias Boudinot, Washington's director of intelligence.

When her husband died, Lydia opened a store for making burial clothes. When she died at the age of sixty, she left her five children an estate worth 1,628 pounds, 17 shillings, and 9 pence.

Her obituary read, "She supported her family in a profession which extended her sympathy to the poor and the wealthy."

At that time in history, it is said that a woman's name appeared in the newspaper only once—at her death. Lydia's name appeared twice. The newspaper gave public recognition to the Quaker woman who, in the role of a spy, saved Washington's army from British defeat.

Deborah Sampson
Private

1.
A Hard Life

Deborah Sampson's father died when she was five years old. Her mother could not feed and clothe their seven children. Deborah was bound out to an elderly relative, meaning she worked for room and board. The older children were bound out to other families.

When Deborah was ten, the elderly relative died. She was then bound out to an old, sick widow. The situation came to the attention of a church deacon who felt Deborah was too young to handle housework and nursing. He arranged to have her work in his house.

The Thomases had one son. A tutor came to their home to give young Thomas his lessons. When Deborah finished her duties, Mrs. Thomas allowed her to listen in on their son's lessons. Deborah wanted an education and hoped one day she could learn enough to become a teacher.

In the attic of the Thomas farmhouse where Deborah slept, she lay on her pallet of cornhusks and daydreamed. The Revolutionary War was going on, and Deborah dreamed of becoming a soldier. At eighteen, she would be freed from her work with the Thomas family, and she could strike out on her own.

2.

The Soldier

One spring night eighteen-year-old Deborah Sampson cut her hair and dressed in men's clothing. She had secretly sewn the outfit from homespun. Then she disappeared from where she lived in Middleborough, Massachusetts.

She walked over fifty miles until she reached Bellingham, Rhode Island. There, she felt no one would recognize her. She enlisted in the Fourth M a s s a c h u s e t t s Regiment of the Continental Army.

She signed her name as Robert Shurtleff, a common name in that area.

Back in Middleborough, Deborah had seen village recruiters waving colorful flags. She listened to drummers and fifers playing marching tunes. No doubt it was then she decided to follow her dream of becoming a soldier.

Deborah knew the military life would not be easy, but she was used to hard work. She performed her duties well.

No one suspected she was a woman. At five feet, seven inches, she was as tall as some of the other soldiers. Too, she had large facial features for a woman. It was not a problem that she had no beard. Boys could sign up at age fourteen, so many did not have beards.

Strong from years of hard work, she did as well as the men on the long march along the

Hudson River in New York. Their first battle came as a surprise, and the regiment had no time to get into formation. They knelt and returned fire until the British brought out their bayonets. Deborah's comrades later said she fired until the battle became hand-to-hand. Then she swung her bayoneted musket at close quarters.

3.
Secret Revealed

The Patriots won the skirmish, but Private Shurtleff received a saber slash across the side of her head. She was lucky it was not serious. The doctor could treat her head wound without discovering Robert was really Deborah.

By now the war was actually over, but the

peace treaty was being formed in Paris, France. It took a long time for a ship to cross the Atlantic Ocean. word of the peace treaty had not yet reached the colonies. Fighting continued in some areas.

A Tory force ambushed Deborah's regiment near Long Island Sound. All in the troop suffered injury fighting their way out. Deborah took a musket ball to the thigh. This time she could not fool a doctor. It is said, she crawled off into the nearby woods and removed the bullet herself.

Deborah knew she could not keep her secret forever, but she hoped to finish her time in the army before the truth came out. When an illness with fever broke out in Philadelphia, Deborah became ill and had to be hospitalized.

Dr. Barnabas Binney discovered her secret. He was a kind man and did not want to betray her, but he felt it was his duty to tell her commanding officer.

Private Robert Shurtleff received an honorable discharge. She had served as a soldier for a year and a half.

4.
Life as a Citizen

After her discharge, Deborah did not return to Middleborough. Her enlistment in the army became known and her church did not approve. In that day and time it was unacceptable for a woman to wear men's clothing. And it was unheard of for a woman to go to war. The general opinion was that a woman's place was in the home.

Deborah went to live with her mother's sister

and her husband. There she met and married Benjamin Gannett, a farmer. The couple had three children. Records show they were very poor.

It was probably due to the family's need for money that Deborah began a speaking tour. Herbert Mann wrote a book about her life as a soldier. He asked her to speak in New England and New York, where he sold tickets for twenty-five cents each. Deborah wore a Continental soldier's uniform when she talked about her war experiences. As she toured, she saw officers she served under in the war.

"They treated me with every mark of respect," she said of their meeting.

The money for speaking and the four dollars a month pension for her army service still did not bring in enough money for the family.

When she and her son became ill, Deborah

wrote to her neighbor, Paul Revere, asking for a loan of ten dollars. Even after the children were grown, the Gannetts had no money. Once Deborah listed all her possessions, including her clothes, to be worth twenty dollars.

After Deborah's death at 66, her ill, 83-year-old husband asked if her pension, which was now eight dollars a month, could be continued until his death. The government granted his request.

Deborah's discharge from the military read, "Deborah showed extraordinary female heroism by discharging the duties of a faithful, gallant soldier."

In World War II, a liberty ship bore her name.

Martha Robertson Bratton
Lady of Compassion

When Martha Robertson from Rowan County, North Carolina, married William Bratton, she came to live in York County, South Carolina. William's father had received a land grant from King George of England.

Even though the British gave his family land, Colonel William Bratton was a staunch Patriot during the Revolutionary War. Governor Rutledge of South Carolina asked William to store their treasured gunpowder near his home. When her husband was away fighting, Martha was in charge of protecting the gunpowder from being stolen by

British soldiers.

One day when Martha and the children were home alone, she received word that the British knew where the gunpowder was stored. They were on their way to steal it.

Martha knew it was better for the ammunition to be destroyed than to have the enemy take possession of it. She made a plan. First she hid her children upstairs. She insisted her little son, who wanted to see everything, get in the chimney behind the fireplace screen and not come out.

With the children safe, she hurried to the secret building beyond their home. Inside, she dipped gunpowder from a keg with an old water dipper. Outside, she made a trail of powder on the ground leading off towards the woods. From the edge of the woods she waited with matches.

When the Redcoats came into sight, she

threw a lighted match on the end of the trail and watched it flame up and run along the black line on the ground.

In moments a loud explosion greeted the arriving soldiers.

As Martha ran toward her house, a soldier caught her arm. He yanked her before Captain Huck, the British officer in command. The officer demanded to know who set the powder on fire.

Martha looked at him without fear. "I did," she said.

"Where is your husband?" he asked.

"He is right where he should be," she said, "fighting for his country."

Her answer made Huck so angry he grabbed a scythe used to cut grain and pushed it against her throat. He threatened to kill her if she did not tell where William Bratton was.

To Martha's surprise, Huck's lieutenant begged for her life. With an even angrier glare at his assistant, Huck threw the scythe aside and demanded she make dinner for him and his men.

Martha did. While she prepared the meal, she listened to the conversation going on in the parlor.

Later that evening when William came home, Martha not only told him why she had to destroy the powder but where the British camped.

Although William knew the British far outnumbered the Patriots, they made a surprise attack. Many British and Tory soldiers lost their lives in that skirmish, including Captain Huck. Others became prisoners of the Patriots.

One of the prisoners was the lieutenant who saved Martha's life. When the Patriots threatened to hang him, he asked to be brought before Mrs. Bratton.

Martha instantly recognized him. Now, she begged for his life. She told her husband she knew him to be an honorable man who kept their children from being motherless.

Martha saw what the war was doing to the hearts of people on both sides. She turned her home into a hospital where she cared for wounded British and American soldiers.

Martha Bratton died in 1816 at their family home, two miles south of York, South Carolina. She is buried beside her husband, Colonel William Bratton.

Catherine (Kate) Moore Barry
Recruiter

Kate Barry's parents, Charles and Mary Moore, were among the first families to come to the Piedmont area of South Carolina. They traveled from Pennsylvania along the Great Wagon Road in a caravan of broad-wheeled, covered Conestoga wagons. Like some of the other pioneers, Charles Moore received a land grant from King George III of England.

At their homesite, now part of Spartanburg County, the Moores found a wilderness rich in elk, buffalo, deer, and Cherokee Indians. Kate chose a spot to plant a few walnuts found in a neighbor's wagon.

When their large country home was completed, they decided to call it Walnut Grove in honor of the walnuts Kate planted.

Kate was the oldest of ten children. The Barrys who came south with the Moores built a home on a neighboring plantation. They had a son named Andrew. At fifteen, Kate married Andrew.

When the Revolutionary War began, Kate's husband became captain of a local militia. As a Patriot, Kate helped in any way she could. She hid food in hollow tree trunks for passing soldiers. She served as a scout, a guide, a messenger, and even a spy.

When she overheard the cruel Tory, "Bloody Bill" Cunningham, was coming toward their area, she wanted to get word to her husband's militia. Her problem was she had no one to watch two-year-old Katie. She came up with the idea of tying little Katie to the bed post with a sheet. Afterwards, she kissed her daughter goodbye and dashed away on her horse, Dolly, to deliver the message.

The story is told that Kate once received a flogging from "Bloody Bill" because she would not tell him were her husband was.

Kate is best known for the help she gave General Daniel Morgan. In 1781, not far from the Barry home, Morgan struggled to keep his small army ahead of the larger force of British general Banastre Tartleton. The Patriot general sent a message to Kate asking her to appeal to her husband for his troops and other Patriots in the area to join him.

Since Andrew was not at home, Kate set out on her own to round up those men she heard had

returned to their homes and ask them to join Morgan.

When the soldiers she recruited joined Morgan's moving army, he stopped running and took a stand to fight at Cowpens. His troops defeated the British.

Kate died in 1823 at seventy-one. She is buried in the Moore family cemetery near the trees that grew from the walnuts she planted as a girl. Americans remember her as a strong courageous woman who made many contributions to the cause for independence.

During the nation's bicentennial in 1976, the Franklin Mint produced a medal praising Kate as one of the "Great Women of the American Revolution." The medal portrays her riding horseback.

The Daughters of the American Revolution, Battle of Cowpens Chapter, erected a marker for Kate Barry on Spartanburg County Road 196 near the I-26 and US 221 interchange.

Walnut Grove Plantation was restored in 1961. Located about eight miles south of the city of Spartanburg, near the marker, it is open to visitors.

Sybil Ludington
Female Paul Revere

Everyone knows about Paul Revere who made his famous ride through the countryside yelling, "The British are coming!" Few know about a sixteen-year-old farm girl who took a similar ride.

On the evening of April 26, 1777, teenager Sybil Ludington was finishing up nighttime duties in her home near Fredericksburg, New York. As she helped get her younger brothers and sisters to bed, she heard a hard knock at the front door.

An exhausted messenger waited to tell Sybil's father the British burned Danbury, Connecticut, twenty-five miles away. The Continentals urgently needed the help of Colonel Ludington's militiamen before the enemy burned Patriot military supplies stored in the area.

Sybil's father explained to the messenger that he had given his soldiers permission to return home to plant their spring crops. They would have to be rounded up.

The winded young man expressed his regrets that he could ride no farther. The colonel wondered how he alone could spread the alarm *and* get the men organized as they arrived.

Sybil saw her father's worry. "I'll go, Father," she said. "I know the countryside, and your men know me."

Colonel Ludington feared for his daughter's safety, but he consented.

Soon Sybil mounted her horse, Star, and

galloped into the night. Carrying a stick to prod
Star and to bang on doors and shutters of
darkened houses, she made her way along narrow,
unmarked roads.

Knowing British spies, wild animals, or
Indians could be around every bend, she urged
Star along worn paths from one village to another.
Patriots she told hurried to tell others.

Sybil returned home by daybreak to find the

regiment gathered in the Ludington yard, ready to face the enemy.

Under the command of Colonel Ludington, the Patriots intercepted the British at Ridgefield and drove them back to their ships on Long Island Sound. The day afterward, the enemy sailed away.

Sybil Ludington received many honors for her heroism. In 1975 a postage stamp with her image was issued as part of the national bicentennial series "Contributor to the Cause."

One hundred fifty years after this heroine's famous ride, a chapter of the Daughters of the American Revolution placed markers along the historic road, pointing out the path she took that night in April.

A statue, sculpted by Anna Hyatt Huntington, stands on New York State Road 52 beside

Gleneida Lake in Carmel. It is called "Sybil Ludington's Ride." The base of the statue reads:

Sybil Ludington
Revolutionary War Heroine
called out the volunteer militia by riding
through the night alone on horseback
at the age of 16, alerting the countryside
to the burning of Danbury, CT, by the British.
Placed by
Enoch Crosby Chapter
DAR
Presented by
Anna Hyatt Huntington
1961

A smaller statue stands in Washington, D.C., in Constitution Memorial Hall at the Daughters of the American Revolution headquarters.

Mary Ludwig Hays
Water Girl

Of all the women who performed heroic deeds during the Revolution, Mary Ludwig Hays is considered the most legendary. Known by her nickname, "Molly Pitcher," Mary Ludwig was born in 1754 and grew up near Trenton, New Jersey. As a teenager, she worked as a servant in the household of Dr. William Irvine in Carlisle, Pennsylvania. There she met and married William Hays, a barber.

At the beginning of the Revolution, Mary's husband enlisted as a gunner in the Pennsylvania artillery. Mary became a camp follower, going first with her husband to the bitter cold of Valley Forge.

It is said she earned her nickname at the Battle of Monmouth in New Jersey. She ran back and forth with a battered pitcher from a stream to the battlefield. Wounded, exhausted soldiers cried out, "Water! Over here, Molly!" "Bring the pitcher over here!" And, finally, "Molly! Pitcher!" This certainly could have happened in the blistering heat of the June battle. It is said the intense heat caused General Washington's horse to collapse.

When Mary's husband fell with a head wound while manning his cannon, Mary stepped forward and took the ramrod from his hands. Punching hard, she rammed the powder down the chamber and fired the cannon. Throughout the remainder of the battle, she endured the grime of the powder, smoke, and dust. Between her duties, she tended her husband's head wound.

Although camp life was hard for family members, it did not bother Mary. She was an exceptionally strong woman. One story tells of her rescue of a wounded soldier who had been left for dead. She carried the man across her shoulders for two miles to her father's dairy farm near Trenton where she nursed him back to health.

For her heroic role, General Washington made Mary a sergeant in the army.

After the war, Mary and William returned to Carlisle, Pennsylvania. They became parents of a son, John. When the boy was around five, his father died. Later Mary married John McCauley. Because the family needed money, Mary worked as a cleaning woman.

In 1822 the Pennsylvania legislature gave Mary a pension for her war service. She received forty dollars a year. After her second husband died, she still cleaned homes and nursed the sick. On Sundays she attended the Lutheran church. She was living with her son and his wife and children when she died at eighty-eight.

Mary Ludwig Hays McCauley received a military funeral in the Old Graveyard at Carlisle. On July 4, 1876, as part of their centennial celebration, the citizens of the town marked her grave with a headstone.

The state of Pennsylvania erected a monument in Carlisle, and the Patriotic Order of the Sons of America placed a cannon and flagstaff nearby. At the base of the Battlefield Monument at Monmouth is a carved figure of Mary in bas-relief. It shows her in action at a cannon with a water bucket near her feet.

Poet Walt Whitman wrote a poem in Mary's memory. He called it "Moll Pitcher."

Margaret Corbin
Captain Molly

Like "Molly Pitcher," Margaret Corbin had a nickname. These two women have often been mistaken for each other. They did have many similar experiences. Each went into battle with her husband. Both men served in the artillery. When their husbands fell alongside their cannons, the wives fired the field pieces in their husbands' places. To add to the confusion, both husbands' names have been recorded as "John." But, Mary Hays left evidence that her husband's name was William, not John.

Margaret Corbin, born Margaret Cochran in

Franklin, Pennsylvania, in 1751, had a tragic childhood. Indians killed her father in a raid when Margaret was about five years old. They took her mother captive and her family never saw her again. Margaret and her brother went to live with their mother's brother. At sixteen she married John Corbin from Virginia.

At the beginning of the Revolution, John enlisted in the Pennsylvania artillery. Margaret went to Fort Washington with her husband as a camp follower. When news came that the British headed toward Camp Washington, John begged Margaret to go home. She refused.

When the British arrived with their cannons, warships, and soldiers far outnumbering the Patriots, Margaret stood beside her husband on the battlefield.

Amid the roar of cannonfire and screams,

Margaret watched John fulfill his duties. With a ramrod he packed powder into the cannon chamber and fired. Then he sponged out the cannon chamber and readied it to fire again.

After an earth-shattering explosion, Margaret saw her husband fall. She knew he was dead, so she stepped up to his duty at the cannon. In spite of her shock and grief, she helped keep the cannon roaring.

By late afternoon the Patriots felt they had no choice but surrender. Suddenly Margaret felt hot balls of iron, called grapeshot, tear through her jaw, arm, and shoulder. She was left for dead on the battlefield.

Later, a doctor gathering the wounded noticed life in her body. He put her on a wagon with the others to go to a hospital in Philadelphia. Margaret was permanently disabled from her wounds.

Records show that Margaret was the first woman to take a soldier's part in the war. She was also the first woman to receive a lifetime military pension for the wounds she suffered in battle.

Margaret received one complete set of clothes when she went with other disabled veterans to the Invalid Regiment stationed at West Point. Of the

286 veterans who received food and lodging there, she is the only woman listed. The men called her "Captain Molly."

As Margaret's condition grew worse, an aide for the Invalid Regiment requested she be allowed to have rum. Women did not generally consume strong drink, but the aide felt it would help to relieve Captain Molly's pain.

When Margaret died around 1800, she was buried on land near West Point. A cedar tree marked her grave. In 1902 the Mary Washington Colonial Chapter of the DAR of New York City placed a stone in Margaret's memory at Holy Rood Church on Fort Washington Avenue. During the Hudson-Fulton Celebration in 1909, the American Scenic and Historic Preservation Society erected a monument in her honor.

In March 1926 the land where Margaret was

buried sold. She was moved to the Military Academy cemetery at West Point. In this new place, the New York state chapter of the Daughters of the American Revolution erected a monument at her grave. The bronze bas-relief, like that at the grave of Mary Hays, shows a woman beside a cannon.

Nancy Ward
Cherokee Beloved Woman

Nancy Ward's Cherokee name was *Nanye-hi*. When Creek Indians killed her husband, Nancy sprang from behind a log to take his place and rally the Cherokees on to victory. She was said to look like a queen. She stood tall, her black hair flowing long and silky.

The Cherokees gave Nancy several names. They called her Beloved Woman, Wild Rose of the Cherokee, Pocahontas of the West, War Woman, and Prophetess.

The title Beloved Woman was reserved for brave and wise women who served their people well. As a Beloved Woman, Nancy was given a voice in the tribal council. The council was one of power. It settled disputes. It could even overrule the chiefs when it appeared the council's decision was best for the tribe.

Although the name War Woman did not fit her appearance, Indian warriors chose to think of her by that name. They asked War Woman to prepare their "black drink" before going into battle.

Nancy worked for peace between the Indians and whites who settled along the Tennessee River. When she heard the British offered to pay Cherokee warriors to attack Patriot settlers, she sent warnings by trader Isaac Thomas to John Sevier and her other white friends. As a result, Patriots destroyed the villages of warriors who harmed Patriots and their families. They did not harm Nancy's Chota clan.

Because Nancy worked with the whites in keeping peace between the Cherokees and settlers, the government appointed commissioners to work with Indians in signing treaties.

After the Revolutionary War, colony leaders appointed Andrew Pickens as an Indian commissioner. He worked in Georgia, South Carolina, and other states. When he invited Indians to his home at Hopewell to talk peace, Nancy Ward came. She offered a passionate plea for peace and gave the commissioners a pipe, the Cherokee symbol of peace. She was present at the signing of "The Treaty of Hopewell." Many believe her actions helped shape the course of history, especially in Tennessee.

Nancy did her best to help her people hold on to their land. After the Hiwassee Purchase of

1819, she left Chota and settled on the Ocoee River near Benton, Tennessee. She operated an inn at Woman Killer Ford until her death in 1822. She is buried nearby.

Her grave lay unmarked until 1923 when the Nancy Ward Chapter of the Daughters of the American Revolution placed a marker on a pyramid of stones at her grave. It reads:

In Memory of
Nancy Ward
Princess and Prophetess
Of the Cherokee Nation
The Pocahontos of Tennessee
The Constant Friend
Of the American Pioneer
Born 1738 – Died 1822

The gravesite is on State Road 411, heading toward Benton, Tennessee. It is on the right side of the highway, approximately three miles northeast of State Road 64. If you are fortunate enough to visit this site, you can also see the graves of her son, Five Killer, and her brother, Longfellow.

Jane Black Thomas
Bold Messenger

Jane Black Thomas, a small, dark-haired woman, moved with her family from Pennsylvania to South Carolina into what they found to be Cherokee country. After a chain of battles, life with the Indians improved. Just as they felt more at peace, the Revolutionary War broke out.

Jane's husband, John, formed the Patriots' Spartan Regiment. Their sons and sons-in-law served in that regiment. Like the men in the family, Jane and her daughters and daughters-in-law became loyal Patriots. They even allowed ammunition to be stored in their two-story log home.

One day while Jane's husband fought in Charleston, word came the British marched toward the Thomas home to seize the ammunition. Captain John Thomas, Jr., and his men gathered as much of the ammunition as they could and carried it to a hiding place in the woods.

Jane, her young son William, son-in-law Josiah Culbertson, and two daughters-in-law remained in the home. When the British arrived, Josiah tried to defend the home.

The women and William passed bullets to Josiah as he fired from one rifle peep hole inside the house and hurried to another.

Thinking more soldiers were inside the house because gunfire came from so many directions, the British pulled back. They regrouped and made another approach.

Jane grabbed a sword and went out to meet

them. Shocked at the behavior of such a small woman, the British withdrew.

Later in the war, Jane's husband and two of their sons became prisoners in a brick jail at Ninety Six. Jane often rode her horse to take them food and care for them. One day she overheard one woman say to another, "Tomorrow night the Tories will surprise the rebels at Cedar Springs."

No doubt Jane felt her heart stop beating. *Their oldest son, John, and her sons-in-law camped with the Spartan Regiment at Cedar Springs.*

Jane rushed to her horse and set out for Cedar Springs. She rode throughout the night, traveling over fifty miles through woods and swamps and across two rivers.

Weak from hunger, she urged her horse on. The next day she arrived in camp and gave the warning.

With her information, the officers made plans. At dusk they built campfires and placed their  bedrolls around them to make the British and Tory soldiers think they had come upon sleeping Patriots.

The trick worked. The enemy soldiers soon found themselves surrounded from all sides.

Jane Thomas's courage made the Patriot victory an easy one.

Until her death at ninety-one, Jane Black Thomas remained a true Patriot.

OTHERS

Mary McClure and her daughter by the same name were both heroines in the American Revolution. While her husband fought in Sumter's militia, Mary did what she could to support the Patriot cause.

One hot day in York, South Carolina, Mary's sons and son-in-law melted pewter plates to make bullets. Without warning, British troops under Captain Christian Huck, a cruel officer of Tarleton's army, swooped down upon them.

The young men tried to hide the pewter and bullet mold, but it was too late. Huck called them "violent rebels" and in a fit of anger dumped the young soldiers in a corncrib to be hanged at sunrise.

When Mrs. McClure protested, one of the soldiers struck her.

Daughter Mary slipped away and rode to Sumter's camp where she told her father and General Sumter about Huck and his men. At once Sumter sent a force to attack Huck.

Mary Musgrove of the South Carolina Up Country nursed the wounded when the Musgrove plantation became the site of a battle. The Musgroves turned their home into a hospital where they cared for injured soldiers from both sides.

Mary's family were considered Tories, but she fell in love with a Patriot, John Ramsey, who lived nearby. It is believed John died in the war.

A white rose grown in Laurens County, South Carolina, bears Mary's name.

Mary Rampage Dillard lived on the Enoree River opposite the Musgrove plantation. She heard that British officer Banastre Tarleton planned to drive General Sumter's militia to Ninety Six and trap the Patriots between his force and that of British general John Cruger.

Mary traveled to General Thomas Sumter's camp and told him what she heard. Because of her quick thinking, Tarleton suffered his first defeat in South Carolina in the battle at Blackstock.

GLOSSARY

adjoining   connected

ambushed   attacked by persons in hiding

ammunition   musket balls, gunpowder, and other
                         supplies for firearms

artillery   large guns; the branch of military that
                         uses large guns

bas-relief   a sculpture in which the figure stands
                         out slightly from the background

battered   worn and damaged by hard use

bayoneted   wounded by a knifelike blade
                         attached to the muzzle of a rifle

betray   be disloyal to

bicentennial   200-year anniversary

black drink   a tea made from yaupon leaves that
                         gave the warriors extra energy

bounded	jumped
boycott	to join together to refuse to buy or use a product
canister	a small box or can used for coffee or tea
caravan	a line of vehicles traveling together
centennial	one hundred years
chink	a narrow opening, as in the wall of a log home; also, something, like a piece of wood, used to fill a chink
commissioner	a leader appointed to perform a certain task
compassion	feelings of concern for others
comrades	fellow soldiers
Conestoga wagon	a large covered wagon used by families in pioneer days to move to another location

Continental Army	American Patriot army during the Revolution; paid soldiers
corncrib	a ventilated building used for storing corn
courier	messenger
crouched	with the body bent low to the floor
DAR	Daughters of the American Revolution
documentation	proof on paper
enlistment	a voluntary period of service in the military
fieldpiece	a large gun used on the battlefield, like a cannon
fifers	persons playing a musical instrument like a flute
flee	hurry away
gallant	brave

gobbler — male turkey

grapeshot — a cluster of small iron balls used as a charge for a cannon

Great Wagon Trail — a wagon road from Philadelphia to the Carolinas used by pioneer families

gunner — a soldier who operates a gun

gunpowder — an explosive powder used in firearms

headquarters — the place from which a military force is controlled

homespun — coarse, handmade cloth

honorable discharge — a formal release from duty after a period of faithful service

intense — strong

intercepted — interrupted and prevented something from happening

invalid	a sick person unable to take care of oneself
keg	a small barrel
legendary	based on stories passed down; famous
legends	stories handed down, believed to be true but not documented
liberty ship	a World War II cargo ship; also used to transport troops
lodging	room and board for overnight
looter	one who plunders or takes by force
memoirs	writing based on personal experience
militia	a volunteer group of soldiers, usually made up of ordinary citizens
minutemen	volunteers who could be ready to go to battle at a minute's notice
mission	a specific task to be accomplished

musket	a long-barreled rifle
muster	to gather or call forth
obituary	the write-up of a death in a newspaper
opposed	resisted; fought against
parliament	a body of government; an assembly of individuals who make laws
parole	a word of honor promised in exchange for freedom
Patriot	one who loves and supports his country; American colonist who fought for freedom from English rule
peace treaty	a formal, written agreement of peace
pellets	small, round, hard masses, like bullets; in this case, dirt
pension	payment made to a person who has fulfilled his military duties

pewter	a dull silver metal made chiefly of tin
pitchfork	a farm tool; a long-handled fork used for pitching hay or straw
plunder	destroy property and take goods by force
pondered	thought deeply about something
protestor	one who speaks out strongly against something
Quaker	a society of Christians who teach peace and oppose war
ramrod	a rod used to push gunpowder into the cannon
rebel	a person who refuses to be controlled
recruiter	someone who asks others to volunteer
Redcoats	the name colonists gave British soldiers because they wore red coats

reeds	tall, slender grass
refuge	shelter from harm
regiment	a military unit
renegade	one who has turned away from principles or restraints of law
retreat	withdraw when faced with danger
room and board	meals and a place to sleep
rowdy	displaying rough behavior
rum	alcoholic beverage; liquor
saber	a heavy sword with a curved blade
scout	a person sent to gather informatoin, usually about the enemy
screeching	high-pitched; piercing
scythe	a farm tool with a long curving blade and curved handle, used to cut grain or tall grass

skirmish	a fight between a small group of soldiers
slave	a person who is property of another and obligated to work for him
smallpox	a contagious disease caused by a virus, which often leaves scars on the skin
staunch	strong in loyalty
stockade	an enclosure like a fort, made of stakes driven into the ground, where prisoners are kept
strategy	a plan of action for a large-scale military operation
symbol	an object that stands for something invisible—like a pipe for peace
Tory	a person living in the colonies who gave allegiance to the king of England during the Revolutionary War

traitor	one who helps the enemy
tramp	heavy steps
tramped	traveled by foot
under arms	in battle order; armed and ready to fight

THINGS TO DO AND THINK ABOUT

1. Heroine Penelope Barker gave a tea party for her friends in Edington, North Carolina. The British poked fun at it, saying it was like the Boston Tea Party the year before. Can you tell one way these two parties were alike and one way they were different?

2. In Nancy Hart's story, the log house in which the Hart family lived had chinks in the walls. Nancy poked the enemy soldiers' rifles to the outside through the chinks. Do you know or can you find out what material was used to bind the logs in the walls together?

3. Other stories of Nancy Hart tell of her acting as a spy for Georgia Patriot forces. It is said she made a raft of logs by tying them with grapevines. She crossed the Savannah River on it and brought back information from enemy camps.

4. When the Marquis de Lafayette visited America in 1825, he told stories of Nancy Hart's bravery. A newspaper published them. It may be surprising to you, but Daniel Boone and Daniel Morgan were her relatives. Her birth name was Ann Morgan.

5. An historical marker on Georgia State Road 17, about ten miles south of Elberton, says Nancy Hart was a "skilled doctor." What sort of medical care do you suppose she gave? Do you think she practiced folk medicine? Find out what that is.

6. Have you ever tried to blow a conch shell? It was said to be the fabled shell trumpet of the Tritons of Greek mythology. Would you like to learn more about them?

7. In Lydia Darragh's story, Major John Andre arranged a meeting of British officers in her home. It is an odd coincidence that both Lydia and Major Andre were spies. Andre was later hanged. His story includes Benedict Arnold, a Patriot traitor, and West Point. You may like to read about Andre by doing a search on the Internet or looking him up in an encyclopedia.

8. It is said that Lydia Darragh traveled through "no man's land" to report the information she overheard in Major Andre's meeting. Would you like to find out what that expression means?

9. When Lydia Darragh died, she left her children an estate worth 1,628 pounds, 17 shillings, and 9 pence. Would you like to figure what this English money would amount to in American dollars and cents?

10. It seems hard to believe that Deborah Sampson could have removed the musket ball from her thigh by herself. It is recorded that an older woman who lived with her in later life said the musket ball was never removed.

11. The length of Sybil Ludington's ride varies in different sources. Some say twenty miles; others say forty. One source puts the distance at twice the ride of Paul Revere. It is said Sybil went through Carmel, Malopec, and around to Kent Cliffs and Farmers Mill, then back home. If you live in New York or visit the state, you can trace her path by following markers on the route. It is recorded, too, that Sybil worked with Enoch Crosby, a famous spy, to help the Patriot cause.

    Whatever her contributions, the citizens of Frederickburg were mighty proud. They changed the name of their village to Ludington.

12. Anna Hyatt Huntington, who sculpted a statue of Sybil Ludington, started Brookgreen Gardens with her husband, Archer Milton Huntington. Brookgreen is located eighteen miles south of Myrtle Beach at Murrells Inlet. You may like to read about Anna Hyatt Huntington in *South Carolina Women* by Idella Bodie and visit the Gardens.

13. Walt Whitman wrote a poem about Mary Ludwig Hays whose nickname was Molly Pitcher. See if you can find his poem called "Moll Pitcher." A public library will have a reference book called *Ranger's Index to Poetry*. You can look up the poem in that book to see where to find it. Check the index under poet's name or poem title.

14. Mary Ludwig Hays and Margaret Corbin helped their husbands fire a cannon, sometimes referred to as a "field piece." Can you explain to your classmates how a cannon is fired? What is a ramrod? A sponge? What kind of ammunition is used?

15. Both Hays and Corbin were honored by statues that included an engraved figure of a woman beside a cannon. The method of sculpture used is called "bas-relief." Can you explain to your classmates what that means? Can you point out an example of bas-relief in your city or another place they might see? Or, can you show a picture of bas-relief?

16. It is interesting to note that Nancy Ward was considered the first Cherokee home economist. That is, she taught how to use food products to the best advantage. She taught how to preserve vegetables and fruits, as well as how to use milk in cooking. Because

of her work in improving the health of her people, an iron skillet was buried with her.

17. Mary Musgrove grew up at Musgrove Plantation, the site of a recently designated South Carolina state park. The Musgrove Mill State Historical Site commemorates the Revolutionary War battle fought there on August 18, 1780. The Daughters of the American Revolution assembled a display on women's role in the war. The park is located off I-26, exit 52.

18. Other women in this series of Revolutionary War heroes and heroines include Emily Geiger, Dicey Langston, and Rebecca Motte. If you have not read these biographies, you may like to do so. Emily and Dicey were teenagers when they performed their courageous deeds. Rebecca was a widow who told Patriot officers to burn her house to keep it out of the enemy's hands.

19. If you'd like to read about more South Carolina women who made lasting contributions during the Revolutionary War, see *South Carolina Women* by Idella Bodie. These individuals include Dorcas Nelson Richardson, Susannah Smith Elliott, and Eliza Yonge Wilkinson.

20. Choose your favorite heroine in this book. Write or tell what you admire about her. What is her outstanding character trait? How does this trait affect her actions?

21. Do you think women were treated fairly during this time period? Why or why not? Choose a woman and work up a monologue. Get in that person's skin and look out at life from her point of view. Share with your classmates how you, as this person, think about your life.

22. Divide into groups and put on skits for your class, based on a scene or scenes from one of these stories. You may make up your own dialogue or conversation based on what you think might have been said.

23. Like the women of the Revolutionary War, people of other wars have gone through difficult times. Do you think someone who experiences hardships in any time or place becomes a stronger, better person because of it? Can you cite an example of when this happened to you or to someone you know or have read about? If you use a person you know, it is not necessary to call his or her name.

SOURCES USED

Barefoot, Daniel W. *Touring South Carolina's Revolutionary War Sites*. Winston-Salem: John F. Blair, 1999.

Coleman, Frank, "Walnut Grove Plantation," *Sandlapper Magazine,* vol.13 (November 1968): 9-13.

Edgar, Walter. *Partisans & Redcoats*. New York: Harper Collins, 2001.

Family Encyclopedia of American History. Pleasantville, NY: Reader's Digest Association, 1975.

Hanaford, Phebe A. *Daughters of America*. Boston: B.B. Russell, 1882.

Internet:
  Various sites through a SEARCH of the women's names. Place names in quotation marks for a cleaner search.

Logan, Mary. *The Part Taken by Women in American History.* Wilmington: Perry-Nalle, 1912.

Raphael, Ray. *A People's History of the American Revolution*. New York: Harper   Collins, 2002.

Rheitt, Barbara B., ed. *Georgia Women, A Celebration*. Atlanta: American Association of University Women, 1976.

Sickels, Eleanor. *In Calico and Crinoline*. New York: Viking, 1951.

Silox-Jarrett. *Heroines of the American Revolution*. Chapel Hill: Green Angel Press, 1998.

Somerville, Mollie, ed. *Women and the American Revolution.* Brookfield, CT: National Society of the Daughters of the American Revolution, 1974.

Tennessee Biographical Dictionary. New York: Somerset Publishers, 1994.

The Uncommon Soldier of the Revolution. Eastern National Park and Monument Association: East Acorn Press, 1986.

Willis, Pat, "Women Helped Win Country's Freedom," *Augusta Chronicle*, 11 September 1997.

Zeinert, Karen. *Those Remarkable Women of the Revolution*. Brookfield, CT: Millbrook Press, 1996.

ABOUT THE AUTHOR

Idella Bodie was born in Ridge Spring, South Carolina. She taught high school English and creative writing for thirty-one years.

Ms. Bodie's first book was published in 1971, and she has been writing books for young readers ever since. This is her twenty-second book.

Ms. Bodie lives in Aiken with her husband Jim. In her spare time, she enjoys reading, gardening, and traveling.

OTHER BOOKS BY IDELLA BODIE:

Carolina Girl: A Writer's Beginning
Ghost in the Capitol
Ghost Tales for Retelling
A Hunt for Life's Extras: The Story of Archibald Rutledge
The Mystery of Edisto Island
The Mystery of the Pirate's Treasure
The Secret of Telfair Inn
South Carolina Women
Stranded!
Trouble at Star Fort
Whopper

"Heroes and Heroines of the American Revolution" Series
The Man Who Loved the Flag
The Secret Message
The Revolutionary Swamp Fox
The Fighting Gamecock
Spunky Revolutionary War Heroine
The Courageous Patriot
Quaker Commander
Brave Black Patriots
The Old Wagoner
The Wizard Owl